Footsteps
to
Bethlehem

Advent time reflections

Bill Merrington

kevin
mayhew

First published in Great Britain in 2018 by Kevin Mayhew Ltd
Buxhall, Stowmarket, Suffolk IP14 3BW
Tel: +44 (0) 1449 737978 Fax: +44 (0) 1449 737834
E-mail: info@kevinmayhew.com

www.kevinmayhew.com

9 8 7 6 5 4 3 2 1 0

ISBN 978 1 84867 961 0
Catalogue No. 1501584

Cover design by Rob Mortonson
© Image used under licence from Shutterstock Inc.
Edited by Linda Ottewell
Typeset by Angela Selfe

Printed and bound in Great Britain

Contents

About the author

Bill initially trained in Forensic Science before becoming ordained in the Church of England. He has worked in city, town, rural and chaplaincy contexts. Bill has specialised in loss issues and has a PhD from Warwick University on the subject of understanding parental child loss cross-culturally.

He has written 12 books on various subjects for children and adults covering grief, pastoral care and counselling, including 7 titles for Kevin Mayhew, the most recent being *Pastoral Care, a practical guide* (1501365).

Bill is a qualified counsellor and supervisor. He has qualifications in PGCHE, Play Therapy, Stress Management, PTSD, Traumatic Loss Events and Hypnotherapy. He is a member of the Fellowship of Academic Higher Academy and has lectured nationally and internationally on counselling, bereavement and resilience issues.

Introduction

Well before the autumn leaves have turned golden brown, you will have no doubt noticed adverts for the Christmas season. Shops will be stocking their potential sales, with all their glitter, to draw people's attention to the holiday season of Christmas.

Whether we like it or not, Advent and Christmas will quickly be upon us, which reflects how quickly life proceeds. In reality it mirrors the journey of every Christian. There is a point where we claim our Christian faith for ourselves and we engage on an encounter with Christ, Christians and the Church. However, before long we realise that we've been Christians for quite some time. We may find ourselves at a point where we are confused about our faith, or unsure where we are heading.

Each day we will look into the life of ordinary people, some young, like Mary and Joseph; others older like Zechariah and Elizabeth, and we will reflect on how they coped with the major events of their lives. We will see how often God gives us a choice in our daily life; to either walk by faith and walk towards the light, or to harden our hearts and stubbornly become fixed (or worse), and retreat from God's light and love. We will see the difference between the Wise Men, who used their wisdom for good, as compared to Herod who turned inward and selfish, to the destruction of many. We will reflect on those who have journeyed in faith to become wise and faithful like Simeon and Anna, who unlike those around them, were able to hold onto their visionary faith through times of great barrenness, persecution and disillusionment.

Day by day we will look at the Christian life and reflect upon our experience, how easy it is to reach a plateau in our relationship with the Church, our prayer life, Scripture or in our service in the community. We will also reflect on our own personality, which can become stubbornly trapped with our own peculiarities and prevent us from becoming the person Christ wants us to be.

If you recognise a degree of frustration, boredom and disillusionment in your faith, then journey this Advent time through the daily readings and reflections, that you might prayerfully seek to journey with Christ to become who he really wants you to be.

How to use this book

- Each day try and imagine yourself as a traveller. As you journey through the readings, reflect on where you are up to on your pilgrimage of transformation.

- Ask God to speak afresh to you before the reading.

- Focus on just one aspect that engages you, either from the Bible reading, or the dialogue that follows.

- Finally, use the suggested prayer to commit yourself to further reflection during the day.

A prayer

Father, the word Emmanuel reminds me
that you are the God who journeys with me.
Thank you for coming into my life and journeying
with me this far.
Lord, I acknowledge that there have been times when I
have got lost,
or failed to follow the map that you have given me,
or simply have become content with where I am,
and how I have become.
I pray this Advent time that you might stir me up,
that I might seek to be more transformed into your image.
Lord, help me to be honest with myself,
yet have the faith to step forward into the unknown,
trusting that you are not only with me,
but will be there to meet me at the end of my journey.
I pray this in Jesus' name, who has journeyed before me
and left me footprints that I might follow.
Amen.

Day 1

Genesis 1:1-5, 27-31

In the beginning there was nothing. Just pause and ponder on that thought. Nothingness. This was not like a piece of black coal or iron ore waiting to be transformed. Nothingness is not even a vacuum that is trying to keep something out. Only if we can begin to grasp what this means will we realise the power that lay in the first words that God spoke. Whether we want to relate this to the big bang theory and black holes or see it totally as a mind-blowing narrative, the message is the same: out of God's voice came life. The narrative account then unfolds from this point onwards. The godly thread of creativity spreads right throughout the history of time as we know it. It is at this point of time along the thread that we find ourselves.

We are just as dependent upon the breath of God now as at the beginning. Nothing in one sense has changed; it still all hangs from God's 'giveness'. This is the starting point of Advent. It begins with God speaking through an angel and ends with God's presence fully on earth. During each step in between, we see God's Spirit working through his creativity. Alas, not everyone had eyes to see this, but we will encounter faithful individuals like Zechariah, Elizabeth, Mary, Joseph, Simeon, Anna and the nameless rich of the Wise Men and the poor of the shepherds, who in their own unique way glimpsed God at work.

How many times have you been on a road where there is a sign warning of men at work, but as you drive by you see cranes and trucks standing still with no workmen to be seen anywhere? Yet strangely, one day you can drive along the same road as before and you notice the roadworks are finished, with no diggers in sight, just a smooth complete highway that you appreciate and benefit from.

It can be easy to think the same about God at work. We can look but fail to see his action or involvement in our lives or the world. How many people thought this 2000 years ago at the time of Christ's birth? Perhaps they were living in the village right next to Bethlehem, yet were unaware of God at work. Life just went on as normal with no sign of God's angels or Holy Spirit but for those who were faithful, prayerful and expectant, the wonder of God's creative love was waiting for them. Could this be our journey this Advent?

God is already present, as he has made us in his image. Could we discover something more of God through the scriptures of the Christmas narrative? And perhaps by journeying together, we might discover what his Spirit is doing right now in our own lives.

Reflection

Sit in total silence, still your breath, calm your heart, be aware of sight, hearing, touch, smell and taste that pervade your daily life and only then, ask yourself:

- Where does your life come from?

- Acknowledge before your Creator the fragility of your life.

- Give thanks that all of life is but a gift from God.

Prayer

Lord, open my eyes to your presence in my life.
May I see you in every breath that I take,
may I open my eyes and hear you at work.
Open up my heart, so I may be ready
for that which you have in store for me.
Amen.

Day 2

At the beginning of the Bible we are told that God wanted to have a relationship with his creation, and especially with humankind.

'Where are you?'

There is a fundamental question over the heart of our Christian journey. This is not usually a location, but is related to the emotional and spiritual condition of a person's well-being. For Adam and Eve, it was their guilt and shame that caused them to hide away. Today, in our busy lifestyles, we can easily become unaware of our personal emotional and spiritual condition. Without realising it, people can live lives hidden amongst the trees of the garden. They find themselves disconnected from themselves and those around them.

At the heart of the Christian message is the belief that people are special. They have the right to have their own 'needs' met. However, if a person fails to recognise their needs, they remain disconnected with themselves and those around them. As we discover our own 'connectedness' with God, others and ourselves, we are called to speak out on God's behalf.

'Where are you?' is the beginning of God's question to us. What was it that God was asking in this question? It incorporates three aspects:

Firstly, where are you in relation to yourself? Adam was ill at ease with himself as he came to the realisation that all was not well.

'Adam, where are you? Are you at peace with yourself? Do you know who you are, do you know what you have done, and do you know where you are going?'

Secondly, God is asking, where are you in relationship to others? We quickly discover that Adam and Eve are not at ease with one another. Adam blames the woman, and Eve blames the snake. There is a common theme within communities, where relationships break down and we fail to take individual responsibility. The outcome is that we seek to find a scapegoat to escape our conscience. This disharmony quickly spills over to everything around us, isolating us from our community and environment.

'Adam, where are you in relationship to Eve, to those around you?'

Thirdly, God is enquiring whether we know where we are in relationship to him. Adam hides because he's not just guilty, but is also ashamed of himself. This shame comes about only because he has something much higher to compare himself with. Here, right and wrong, moral standards and the consequences of our actions manifest themselves.

'Adam, where are you in relation to me? What have you done to our relationship?'

Now outside the garden, Adam knows he is not what he could have been and he must now live with the consequences of his actions. He is now on a journey of how to re-find himself, to restore his relationship with those around him and to bring harmony to his friendship with his Creator. It is in this complex story that you need to begin your Advent story, engaging with your emotional and spiritual health check.

Reflection

How would you answer the question God put to Adam?

- Where are you in relation to yourself?

- Where are you in relation to others?

- Where are you in relation to God?

Prayer

Lord, thank you that you are asking me this question,
for it shows that you are longing to bring me home.
Help me to be honest about myself,
that I might begin my journey afresh with you,
with those around me and with myself.
Amen.

Day 3

Matthew 1:1-3, 16, 17

You can only begin a journey by recognising and accepting where you are at a particular moment in time. What can help is to look back and see how your journey has brought you to this point in time.

The birth of Jesus in all four Gospels begins by looking backwards. Chapter one of Matthew begins with a genealogy, which reminds us that Jesus did not just appear but came out of a family heritage. There are forty fathers listed, without mentioning the mothers and grandparents who all influenced the family line.

Mark's Gospel begins by reminding us of a prophecy from Isaiah that God is actively preparing the way forward. For Jesus, it was his cousin John, influencing events that would shape and direct Jesus' ministry.

Luke initially tells us that a careful account has been made of the past, for with God nothing is forgotten. This orderly account provides the most detail of Jesus' beginnings. There are eighty verses drawing our attention to characters that played a part in Jesus' initiation into life.

John pronounces that all things begin with God: 'Without him, not one thing came into being' (John 1:3). John's prologue is a loud declaration that God's light has been at work for the history of time. Whether or not you can see God in your past, John assures us that he has been there. From early in Jesus' life, he seemed to recognise his heritage. God the Father was at work in his life, he had been placed within a particular family at a time in history with all its complexities. We never hear Jesus complaining to the Father about his parents, or the fact that his childhood was one of being a refugee, constantly travelling, or having been placed in a time of Roman occupation. This was the context that God the Father placed him into, and it was from there that Jesus embarked on his calling and ministry.

If the heritage of Jesus is so important and significant, perhaps your own life should also require some recognition of where you have come from. One can only move forward in life from where you are at the present. This is your crucible, where you grind out your learning. Taking stock of where you have come from involves recognising your genetic make-up, your cultural setting, your parentage, your childhood experiences and the decisions you have made that have resulted in you reaching this point in time.

Wearing glasses leaves visible marks on the nose, whereas contact lenses are so invisible that you can even forget you are wearing them. This 'comfortableness' fools us into thinking we don't actually have weak eyes. The shock comes when, after the removal of the lenses, everything is seen in a different light. Going back to glasses and looking through the framed glass is a reminder of imperfect vision. It is only through accepting the eyes – that have been given and the tools found, that enables looking forward with a sense of clarity.

Reflection

- How aware are you of your heritage and family tree?
- Who has played a significant part in your early life?
- Can you accept your beginnings?

Prayer

Father, in the vastness of time and space,
I find myself at this place;
at this moment help me to be honest about my identity,
especially the parts that I have had no control over.
May I learn to be kind to myself,
and from my heritage and inherited abilities,
seek to make the most of what you have given me.
Amen.

Day 4

Luke 1:1-4

When Luke tells us he has written an orderly account, what he means is that he has written a chronological description of the life of Christ. It is, however, Luke's story, seen from his perspective only, although he incorporates other people's views as he journeys in the account. We also have Matthew, Mark and John's accounts of Jesus' life. Each is a story in itself, seen from a different perspective. It is as if we are looking through differing lenses, giving a new angle and view of Jesus himself and how others perceive him.

It is not just the four Gospels that tell us the story. In fact, the whole Bible is a storybook about how God relates to humankind and how humankind relates to itself. Why is it that God has bestowed his message to us in a story form? Perhaps it's the same reason why so many people love 'soaps'. Human beings spend their time interpreting their lives. These lives or stories are made up of connecting events in a particular sequence over time. The way we understand these events creates a plot to the story. We all have our own stories to tell which involve our struggles, abilities, relationships, interests, achievements and failures.

Stories draw our attention and they get us thinking. They also tell us something about the world that we live in, particularly of how people function. They give shape to our experience and tell us how the world works.

It is in sharing stories that our feelings of joy, love, excitement, shame, fear, and rejection are expressed and given context. It reminds us that our discoveries are not limited to ourselves but are, in fact, shared with others.

If you bump into someone, you introduce yourself and you tell a short story about yourself. It isn't the whole story but is a part of a story that you have chosen to share. It may well be true, although it may not contain the whole truth. Sometimes we can develop what is called 'a thin story', which appears to focus on the negative aspect of our lives and misses out on the positive, joyful experiences of life.

However you perceive your story at this point in time, the reality is that it is only one interpretation. The reality is that the 'title' of your book has not yet been written and the remaining chapters of your life are yet to be formed. When Matthew, Mark, Luke and John began their journey with Jesus, they could not have predicted how their story would develop. What we do know is that we are just the same as all the characters in the Gospels, where they are each given a choice of how to respond to the future. We too find ourselves at a crossroads; the next chapter is yet to be written. Will we allow Christ to shape it with us as we journey into the unknown?

Reflection

At this point in time, if you were going to write an autobiography:

- What would your storybook about your life be called?

- How many chapters have you had so far? (This may be chronological or may be based upon certain events or people in your life.)

- Are you at the beginning, middle or end of a chapter in your life? (What reasons do you give to come to that conclusion?)

- What would you like to leave behind from the last chapter?

- What is it that you would like to bring with you into your future?

- How would God write your story?

Prayer

Jesus, forgive me that sometimes I see my story from a negative perspective
and ignore all the moments of wonder that you have placed within my life.
Thank you that you have been with me like a character in a book
and that you will journey with me right to the very final page of my story.
Give me the faith and courage to embark on the next part of my story,
knowing that you can always help me to rewrite the future.
For Jesus' sake.
Amen.

Day 5

Luke 1:5-7

When the Angel Gabriel appeared to Mary and gave her an amazing message, it naturally came as a shock. However, six months before this event, God was already at work while Mary and Joseph were totally unaware. They were just getting on with their lives. It was a time of discouragement for the faithful, due to Herod powerfully controlling and dictating how people lived.

In a quiet part of a village, an elderly, faithful couple named Zechariah and Elizabeth were getting on with their lives. Being unable to conceive a child in such a culture would not have been easy for either of them. Yet the Scriptures tell us that despite their anxiety, they were faithful. Their example is similar to Joseph's in the Old Testament, whose story led to considerable suffering, yet the Psalmist tells us that he overcame the 'iron chain' around his neck, rather than the chain digging into him making him bitter and resentful (Psalm 105:18). However, in the background, (unknown to all), God was at work.

Zechariah and Elizabeth represent to us someone who is grappling with their faith, seeking to move forward, while at the same time carrying questions and burdens which constantly challenge their faith. As Christians, we are called to be faithful and to be righteous, while at the same time recognising that we have not yet been fully transformed.

Can you imagine what it would have been like to have been a fly on the wall in the home of Zechariah and Elizabeth, hearing their conversations about faith, about life and about how to be faithful, even when it seemed God had not brought them that which they were longing for? Yet it is clear that Zechariah and Elizabeth held on to the belief that God was still at work in their lives.

When you look back at your story, you need faith to believe that there has always been a thin red line of Christ's presence, running through your life. This is a fundamental foundation stone to the Christian faith. It is the belief that God has made us and seeks to work in our lives, regardless of whether we perceive it or not. It is this kind of attitude that prevented Zechariah and Elizabeth from turning bitter and hindering their journey of righteousness.

Reflection

- Can you sit with God knowing that there are questions at present that you have no answers to?

- Can you progress with God while carrying disappointments?

- What is it that you learn from your faith at such times?

Prayer

Lord, I feel like sitting in your crucible,
a place of pain and learning.
Please help me to see the heavenly in my situation
and seek to bring a resurrection perspective
out of all my situations.
Amen.

Day 6

Luke 1:8-10

Whether it is on TV, in newsagents or petrol garages, you can't go far before you're faced with the idea of luck and chance in your life. Whether you like it or not, the lotto (in one form or another) is always near at hand. It might seem strange to see Zechariah engaging in an activity of chance (not gambing). The religious leaders drew lots to see whose turn it was to represent them in the temple. Perhaps chance is more prominent in our lives than we think. We begin life as a baby, trying to make sense of the world through our own experience. Bit by bit we begin to form assumptions of life, which gives us confidence to explore the world. Every morning before we get out of bed, we make thousands of subconscious assumptions about life; otherwise we would be a nervous wreck and stay in bed all day. As our assumptions of life are challenged or fail, we have to reprocess our thinking and come to new conclusions of life.

What were Zechariah's assumptions? Was it really chance that led Zechariah to the temple to meet the angel? Whether the shortest or longest straw fell to Zechariah, God could have arranged a quiet place for him to meet the angel. As Christians, we live in a world where God allows us wonderful and fearful freedom.

The 'lotto' is always around us with germs, viruses and the unpredictable waiting to happen. Understandably, most humans (and that includes Christians), go through life pretending that life is a little more secure than it is. It allows us the confidence to explore and create, but when the unexpected occurs, it upsets the 'apple cart' of our belief system.

So what is the advantage in being a Christian? Are we not also told that God knows all things? That a sparrow doesn't fall without God knowing? Note that it does not say that sparrows never fall. It's this 'knowing' that allows Zechariah to go with the flow of life. 'If I'm picked to go to the temple, God will be there and if I'm never picked, surely God will still be with me.' Sooner or later as a Christian, you have to grapple with a world that lives with randomness, yet learn to hold onto the belief that God knows all things. For from the very moment of creation, he seeks to bring order out of chaos. It is in this long-term hope that Christians learn to live with the unpredictable.

Reflection

- As you reflect upon your life, can you see both providence and chance at work?

- How do you cope with the randomness of life?

- Can you hold on to the thin 'red line' of God's presence in your life?

Prayer

Lord, I do not know what is before me, but this I hold
on to,
that you have promised to be with me through all things.
Give me the courage to believe this,
even when the unexpected occurs.
Amen.

Day 7

Luke 1:11

Prayer is a wonderful gift that God has given us, but does your prayer life change as you grow in your faithful relationship with God? A prayer I was taught as a child, (apart from the Lord's Prayer) was: 'Lord, wash me out like a petrol tank, wash out the old petrol that makes me splutter and fill me with your new petrol from the Holy Spirit, that I might produce the fruit of the Spirit of love, joy and peace.' This is a prayer that still applies today, but sometimes, things we once prayed for, we would now be hesitant to pray today. It mirrors our relationships, for after all, one's prayer life is simply a relational conversation with God. There are various types of relationships we engage with.

Firstly, 'Contractual Bond' relationships are a mutual agreement between two or more parties, as seen in a marriage in a registry office. Here, two people make an agreement in law together but it only takes one person to end such an agreement.

Secondly, 'Sacred Bond' relationships, such as between a parent and child. Can we ever not be the parent? Although children may see their bond more as a contractual one, in which they only maintain it when they are getting something out of the relationship.

You then have 'Crescive Bond' relationships, where two people become so entwined that they become more and more alike. Here, their thinking and behaviour seem to become synchronised. Many marriages mirror this kind of union. Can you see your prayer life following a similar pattern? You begin rather formulaically, as you tend to ask God for far more than you give back. There is this expectation that it is an agreement where you ask and God gives. Then, there's a stage where you settle in your prayer life, such that it becomes regular and natural. It's something that you do and you would struggle to think of life without it.

Finally, your prayer life can be so in tune with God that you can simply sit with God. Here, asking for things becomes less necessary; after all, God knows the desires of your heart. The incense in some churches is the symbolic representation of the prayers of the people. Some of us use many words, while others can be content that God already knows. Whichever is your preference, your prayer life will reflect your relationship with God. Woody Allen said that marriage is like a shark; it has to keep moving forwards or it will die. (He also said he had a few dead sharks on his hands!) But it should also be true of our prayer life. A healthy relationship is always moving forwards.

Reflection

- We are not told what Zechariah prayed in the temple. If you had his story, what would you have prayed?

- How are your prayers different today, compared to the past?

- Does your prayer life reflect a growing relationship with God?

Prayer

Our Father, which art in heaven,
hallowed be thy name.
Thy kingdom come.
Thy will be done in earth,
as it is in heaven.
Give us this day our daily bread.
And forgive us our trespasses,
as we forgive those that trespass against us.
And lead us not into temptation,
but deliver us from evil.
For thine is the kingdom,
the power and the glory,
for ever and ever.
Amen.

Day 8

Philippians 4:6, 7

Did you ever wonder why God did not just leave Zechariah and Elizabeth alone? After all, although they had prayed for a child, they are now old and adjusted to the reality of the situation. What does this tell us about God? Any involvement with God leads to what can be called a 'heavenly encounter'. When you take God totally away from the encounter, you are left with what we call 'hell'. However, if we seek heaven, then we need to take this higher focus into the present situation. Life is not just a trial run but the real thing. Jesus constantly reminds us that the kingdom of heaven is now in the midst of us.

If we are to be transformed then we need to begin practising heaven on a daily basis. This echoes the Lord's Prayer that reminds us 'on earth as it is in heaven'. Since God wants to continue to journey with your heavenly encounter on earth, is he going to let you settle for second best? This doesn't mean that you will get what you desire, but it does mean that God will nudge you into growth. What a challenge of growth it was for Zechariah and Elizabeth.

'How can I believe this?'

Zechariah's God appeared to be too small, as his faith had become complacent. His God was based on his past experience and not the hope of the future. As we journey to Christmas, we begin by taking stock of our lives. After all, you don't buy presents that you already have. Christmas begins with an assessment of where we've got up to. The question we have to ask ourselves is, 'Have I plateaued in my faith?' The book of Philippians assures us that our anxieties can be reduced if we know that there is a God who loves us and listens to our prayers.

Reflection

- What aspects of your life have you neglected?

- Is God nudging you about an aspect of your life?

- During the next year, what areas of your life would you like to grow in?

Prayer

Lord, there are some visions and dreams I've seen fulfilled, others I have let go of and moved on from.
This I accept, but please keep nudging me from my complacency,
as I know my journey is not yet complete.
Amen.

Day 9

Luke 1:10

Before Elizabeth and Zechariah's story develops, let's pause and try and imagine what it was like to be this couple. Elizabeth and Zechariah were no different from the rest of us on this earth. They had basic needs along with hopes and desires. We all have physical needs of air, food, sleep and protection. Emotionally we desire affection, attention, approval, encouragement, appreciation and respect. One can only suspect that it was no different in historical Jewish society for this couple to feel incomplete without a child. Unlike today, it was seen as a weakness not to have children.

What do we do as Christians when our needs are not fully met? Some develop a negative spirit, while others fall away from their faith. What of this couple? It seems that they still remained faithful. They expressed their concerns to God through prayer, as the angel reminds us (Luke1:13). They continued to be active in caring for others, with Zechariah playing his role as a priest. However, regardless of how much our needs are met, God tells us: 'Give and it will be given to you' (Luke 6:38). This refers to love, judgement and forgiveness.

'You reap whatever you sow.' (Galatians 6:7)

'It is more blessed to give than to receive.' (Acts 20:35)

Could this couple be an example of how to make the most of what we have? Sometimes we have to come to a point of acceptance before we are ready to move on.

What is significant in Luke's account is that he tells us that the people came together to pray. It is hard to accept tough aspects of life when we are alone. Problems often cause us to isolate ourselves and withdraw into ourselves. As difficult as it must have been, Zechariah and Elizabeth chose not to isolate themselves and still engaged with the community.

Reflection

- Are there aspects of your life that you have come to terms with?

- Do you continue to talk to God about your concerns?

- Are you still active in God's work, regardless of your disappointments?

Prayer

Lord, help me to continue to mourn and express my feelings to you.
Protect me from bitterness and enable me to continue to be faithful,
as I seek to serve and give, rather than take.
Help me not to push people away but value their support.
Amen.

Day 10

Luke 1:11-17

We hope according to our dreams,
but live according to our fears.
(Michel Foucault)

Isn't it strange that we spend so much time praying, yet we don't expect God to respond? So often in Scripture we are told that when an angel appears, people feel afraid. I guess we would all be surprised if we saw an angelic messenger that is spirit, yet can appear in human form. 'Do not be afraid' is a recurring theme in Scripture. This phrase doesn't occur often enough for us to have a verse for every day of the year but enough times to give us a godly message. Fear confines and hinders us; it's like a straitjacket that constricts our movements.

Being brought up as a child with an aggressive grandfather, a mother who was a nervous wreck, a father who travelled away from home and having a gentle grandmother dying of cancer, (lying in a bed in the lounge) is enough to make any child full of fear. The fear can still lurk nearby, always ready to pop out and frustrate. But the discovery of a God who knows your name, who loves you and has committed himself to you can enable this fear to be cast out.

Scripture tells us that 'perfect loves casts out fear' (1 John 4:18). When children are surrounded by love, they are able to feel secure enough to explore their surroundings and be adventurous. As adults we need to hold onto this concept. We may no longer have the security of the wider family around us, but holding on to God's love can provide the confidence we need for what lies ahead. However, this only applies if you choose to live in this belief. It is as we daily live within the principles of our faith that we too can experience, as the angel put it, 'joy and gladness' (verse 14).

Reflection

- Can you recognise what your fears focus upon?

- What helps you to balance your fears and hopes?

- If an angel spoke the words 'do not be afraid', what would it mean to you?

Prayer

Father, we know that some fears help us to be safe and aware of danger.
But help us to recognise unhelpful fears that bind and frustrate us.
Give us the courage to let your light shine upon these shadowy fears
and allow us to live more in our hopes.
Amen.

Day 11

Luke 1:18-20

'How can I be sure?' asked Zechariah. After all, he had been faithful in his religious duties all his life. Yet, for many years, he carried his cross of not having a child. Grappling with his belief in God, and a disappointed wife, it was no wonder he was confused when the angel addressed him.

Perhaps it is a question you have asked? How can I be sure of my faith? The short answer is that you can't. However, it is not the only thing in life that we can't be sure of. Right from birth we begin to learn from our caregivers. When we cry, we learn we are cared for by the way our caregivers treat us. This begins to teach us how the world works. We begin to make assumptions about life from our early childhood experiences, piecing them together like a jigsaw. Bit by bit we make more assumptions about life from these encounters. It is only by subconsciously accepting thousands of assumptions that we are able to live a relatively calm life with low anxiety.

I lived in an old vicarage where the lounge had minor cracks in two corners of the ceiling. One day there was a cracking noise and the whole ceiling collapsed. The assumption that ceilings were safe had been shattered and led to me constantly looking up to check its safety. Despite such a difficult experience, it is possible to live with the assumption (and faith) that ceilings are on the whole worthwhile! Could your Christian faith be similar?

You build your faith perhaps first by the witness of others, then on God's Word and through worship, followed by your own experience of God with the Holy Spirit guiding you as you walk through life. This journey will inevitably raise moments when you are challenged with your assumptions. For Zechariah, his 'falling ceiling' was being childless. The question is: Do you live in your doubts or in your faith beliefs? There are consequences with your choices. For Zechariah, his doubting led to a period of silence (verse 20). Others can find themselves becoming disillusioned or bitter or resentful. No one can go through life without faith challenges, but you can choose to live with what you do know, rather than what you don't.

Reflection

- What helps you to maintain your faith?
- How important is church? Bible reading? Prayer? Fellowship with other Christians? Serving others? Witnessing your faith?

Prayer

Lord, help me to be thankful for the years of your goodness in my life.

I acknowledge that there have been challenging times,
moments when I have been lost and disillusioned,
but help me to live in what I know from your Word,
allowing this belief to make me strong and hopeful.
Amen.

Day 12

Luke 1:21-23

'Where is Zechariah?' enquired the faithful outside the temple. It wasn't as if the crowd didn't know where he was. It was rather that they were confused as to what he was doing in the temple. It doesn't seem that the angel took all of that time, so what was Zechariah doing? One can only assume, now that he was muted for a period of time, that he was reflecting upon the situation. The benefit of a time of silence and reflection runs throughout the Bible. The prophets would often withdraw from the community to have time to listen to God. As Elijah found, God's voice was not in all the noise and flashing lights of nature, but rather in the still, small, calm voice (1 Kings 19:11, 12).

Finding a time to be alone allows for a dynamic conversation to take place with two sources. First, it allows us to be able to hear ourselves speak. We can be so busy as we head towards Christmas, in this full-on media technological world, that we hardly get time to think. Reflection provides an opportunity to notice what your mind is focusing on, to pay attention to your emotions. Secondly, it is from this self-awareness that you can bring yourself fully to God. Now, your engagement with God can be genuine and relevant, rather than habitual or religiously ritualistic. This allows you to bring your body, mind and soul together.

What prevents an individual from being harmonised is when your basic needs are not met. This leads to frustration, anxiety and dissatisfaction. Christians can easily become bitter and resentful when their expectations appear not to be fulfilled. Being still before God, acknowledging your position before him, how can you not see that in your faith in God, he has provided for your ultimate needs?

> 'Blessed are the poor in spirit for theirs is the kingdom of God.' (Matthew 5:3)

If we can see and recognise this, we will find satisfaction, contentment, and a feeling of being loved and cared for. I wonder if Zechariah laughed at himself? Here he is, dumbstruck, so many years of speaking without really understanding. Now humbled in his old age, amazed that God should even be aware of him, let alone consider him. Yet he discovered a God who knew him.

Reflection

In a still moment:

- What does it mean to you that God is aware of you?

- How do you find God speaking to you?

- Can you recognise your own different voices speaking to you?

- Which voice dominates and which hardly gets a hearing?

Prayer

Lord, whether I am a young Zechariah full of hope,
or weary after the years of hoping and frustrations,
I still pause and acknowledge your greatness
and the gift of life you have placed within me.
As a child, I hold onto the belief that you are my
loving Father.
Amen.

Day 13
Luke 1:26-38

Three times we are told that Mary was a virgin. Luke gives us a reminder of the message of the incarnation of God, who seeks a relational union between himself and humankind. We can't fully comprehend why God chose Mary, except we're told twice that she was 'highly favoured' and very willing to be a servant. Mary lived up to this in her motherhood of Jesus and her commitment to her son right to the very end and beyond.

What we do know is that the miracle was promised of a union between the Holy Spirit and Mary. Here, for the first time since the beginning of the creation of humankind, God's presence was totally integrated in a human being. Humans were made in God's image and many prophets of the past had experienced the Holy Spirit coming upon them like a cloak or covering, but no one had experienced a union with God as Mary experienced it. Why is this significant? For Luke, all that follows in the Gospel story unfolds from this one announcement. Without God's pure and holy presence, how could Jesus be the only 'begotten' son? How else could Jesus represent both humankind and God?

We all know something of the struggle within us to find fulfilment and peace in life. Living on this planet 'home alone' creates a loneliness that today is almost an epidemic and causes considerable pain. But here is a message that God can come close and work with us from within ourselves.

This miracle was a surprise to many. Jews believed that God was so omnipotent that he was seen as distant, while the Gentiles believed that the spirit and flesh could not be mixed. It's no different from today in our scientific world that fails to be open to the miraculous and the unknown.

Mary's acceptance was a contrast to Zechariah who struggled to believe in a normal human birth to his wife. Mary, on the other hand, had what was called 'searching faith', where she asked the angel, 'How could this be?' The angel explained and encouraged Mary with the news of Elizabeth's pregnancy. Mary revealed her faith, echoing the voice of the angel, 'Nothing is impossible for God.'

Advent is a time to take stock of the facts of the angel Gabriel's message. God has come close to humankind in visiting an ordinary town like Bethlehem. God's love and holiness are available to those who believe in him, and God has chosen to work in ordinary human beings. Can this be true for you?

Reflection

- How do you balance the miraculous and the factual scientific approach in your life?

- If God is willing to come so close to another human, what does this tell you about your relationship with him?

- How can you be like Mary and remain 'enquiring' with God?

Prayer

Lord, renew my awareness of your presence on earth.
Help me to be open to your work in my life,
home and community.
Give me the faith of Mary, to act as a child of God,
and in my simple way, be a witness to those around me.
Amen.

Day 14
Luke 1:39-45

Here is a picture of intense intimacy. Elizabeth's baby, so in tune with his mother, that the joy Elizabeth experienced was passed into the womb, to an embryo of John the Baptist, who responded accordingly. We all begin life the same way, within a womb of warmth, food and attention. Once born, everything changes. We will die in minutes if we are not given air, warmth, food and protection. We even know that if we don't receive love and affection, it will impact on our brain development. Bit by bit we begin to form an attachment to our chief caregiver, who begins to teach us how the world works.

In life, we formulate many attachments to people, concepts and ideas. We also hopefully form an attachment to God, who also supplies us with the essentials of life, including acceptance, forgiveness, direction and hope. However, just as humans can vary in their attachment to others from being secure, anxious or avoiding, so your relationship with God can range from secure to insecure.

If your relationship is one of avoidance, you will tend not to depend upon God in daily life. Prayer will seem like a chore, a matter of fact rather than personal. Scripture will be more about the history than the relevance to life today. You won't see a deep need to be close to God.

Your worship might be routine, unemotional, focusing on past events in your Christian life, rather than on God's work today.

If your relationship with God is an anxious one, it will impact on how you pray, read Scripture or relate to God on a daily basis. You will be anxious about your relationship with God, it will oscillate from hot to cold; you might crave a deeper security from God. Your prayer life will focus on emotional needs and you will worry if you think you haven't prayed enough. Your worship might oscillate from emotional and tearful to times of dryness, not feeling connected with other worshippers.

However, if your relationship with God represents security, you will be comfortable with how life turns out, trusting God's involvement. Your relationship with God will seem secure in the belief that he loves you and won't forsake you. This relationship, although based upon how God has revealed his love to you in the past, will also be open to signs of God's kingdom today. Worship will focus on both giving and an openness to receiving. Involvement within a church, despite ups and downs, will represent commitment, reliability and faithfulness.

This attachment to God might be a mirror of how we develop relationships as a child. An anxious relationship with caregivers may now be seen in how we relate to God. A cold and distant relationship with caregivers might equally be seen in how we perceive God. Although the events of the past cannot be changed, we can recognise what our relationship looks like and feels like. From there, we can begin to ponder whether we would like to be more synchronised with God.

Perhaps it's time to stop being envious of Christians in church who seem so secure with God. It might just be a result of their upbringing. In the parable of the talents, Jesus reminds us of what we have been given, rather than what we have never had. It all begins with acknowledging the position of our godly relationship. Only then can we seek to be more synchronised with God in our lives.

> Blessed are those who believe that the
> Lord will fulfil his promises.

Reflection

- Can you see any correlation between your early relationships with caregivers and now with Jesus?

- Are there godly facts that you need to accept and remind yourself of daily?

- How can your relationship with Jesus be more attuned?

Prayer

Father, I am grateful that you know me 'right well'.
You understand my birth and my upbringing,
my culture and environment that I now live in.
Help me to be awakened to your Holy Spirit;
that I may open up closed areas of my life
and continue to be transformed.
Amen.

Day 15

Matthew 1:1-17

Why does Matthew's Gospel begin with this long list? There are a few names that stick out, like Abraham, Isaac, Joseph, Ruth, David and Solomon. But most of the names are far less familiar. What possible significance can they have to your life? After all, it's not your family tree. With the age of technology, searching one's family heritage has become easier and popular. We all want to know something about our roots and heritage.

Matthew's genealogy is important for several reasons. First, it roots Jesus' birth in the context of what God has been doing since creation. Here is the fulfilment of the prophecies of God working through his first promises with Abraham. God chose Abraham and told him he would be faithful and bless the line of Abraham to its completion with the birth of the Messiah. This is why although Jesus brought us the Gospel we follow, we still learn from the Old Testament; it shines a light on the journey of God with his people. The coming of Christ was not a sudden whim by God the Father but a climax from the beginning of his work with humans. This genealogy tells us much more.

Secondly, it tells us that God knows. He is a God of detail who doesn't forget a name. The less prominent names of Asaph, Jotham, Manasseh and Jeconiah are not forgotten by God. He doesn't live in the world of celebrity and fifteen-minute fame. We have a God who knows us by name and records our lives. In a world where so many feel that they are unheard and not cared for, this is a message for our generation.

Thirdly, the genealogy tells us that we have a part to play in his plan. At times it may not be clear, we may even get lost along the way, like so many of the names on this list, but God is still faithful and at work despite our failings. This informs us that at this point of time in the history of humankind, we can make a small difference. We have a part to play that connects us with the past and the future. Just as from Abraham to Joseph, who were not given a map of the whole terrain, we too journey without a complete map, but nevertheless we are called to respond to God today.

However small your part may be, it will one day connect to the whole of God's cosmic plan. And it's in the midst of God's Alpha to Omega plan that he will remember you.

Reflection

- Can I come to terms with my own genealogy, warts and all?

- What can I do today to play my part in God's kingdom plan?

- Can I find peace, finding myself as a name in the middle of a genealogy?

Prayer

Father, thank you for your omnipotence,
that you can hold the created universe in your care.
Yet I know you recognise and want my small contribution.
May I never forget that you know my name.
Amen.

Day 16

Matthew 1:18-25

What must it have been like to be the parents of Jesus, the Son of God? It's hard to get your head around this subject. The Scriptures tell us very little except the incident in the temple when his parents thought Jesus was lost. Parenting can be tough in normal circumstances, but trying to understand the behaviour of a unique child adds another dimension.

The Church has focused heavily upon Mary, the mother, but what about the father, Joseph? We don't hear anything about him in Jesus' adult life, so it is assumed that he must have died at some earlier point. However, this account of Joseph does give us an insight into his character, and why he was chosen for such a task. It tells us that he was faithful to the law of God. Here is a man who worshipped regularly, a prayerful person following the Torah, as best he knew how. Today he would have been a faithful Christian, going to church, part of a home group, reflecting on how to apply Scripture, and active in charitable work.

Secondly, we see that Joseph was sensitive and considerate. He chose to look above the law and seek a graceful response to the predicament he was in. He could have been angry, shamed Mary and made her an outcast in the community. The law gave him this right, but Joseph chose otherwise. He had learnt the wisdom of thinking before speaking and reflecting before taking any action. How many problems in the world could have been resolved if people had followed Joseph's approach?

Finally, we see something even more remarkable in Joseph's dream (verse 20). It doesn't sound much, as we all dream every night. Some dreams are vivid and some more like nonsense, however, most fade by the break of dawn. For Joseph, this experience was something different. The angel enlarged Joseph's understanding of grace one hundredfold. Joseph believed in a message that proclaimed how God could take the worst situation and transform it, resulting in the blessing of many. The dream is summed up in the name he is to give the child: 'God with us'.

This message of how God relates to his people runs throughout Scripture. Whatever the situation, if given to God with faith and obedience, it can lead to a blessing. This is not to say that what Joseph did was easy or without incredible difficulties. We don't know how his family responded to the situation, or the local community with their gossip and accusations. Joseph didn't experience 'God with us' as Mary did, as his life was cut short. Purely from Joseph's situation, what he saw and experienced was a difficult cross to bear. Yet he remained faithful, protecting Mary and the child as they fled to Egypt.

We all have our own unique journey of life and story to share, but we are also all challenged with the same fundamental question: 'Will I believe in a creator God and be faithful to him through all things, regardless of the terrain?'

Reflection

- How do you identify with Joseph?

- What relevance do you give to your dreams?

- Think about having a notebook by your bedside to write down your dreams.

Prayer

Father, open my heart and mind to your presence
in my life.
Help me to follow you from what I have learnt
but also to remain open for you to surprise me.
Whatever the road ahead may look like,
help me to remain faithful and
continue to grow in your grace.
Amen.

Day 17

Matthew 2:1-8

In the church we tend to focus on the story of the Wise Men after the birth of Christ, but in reality, their journey must have begun weeks earlier. The account of a wandering star and foreign Wise Men travelling to discover a baby may seem far-fetched in this modern age. However, we need to remember why Matthew wrote his Gospel. Matthew's consistent message was that the birth of Jesus was not only for the Jews, but also for the nations. The Magi capture this wider dimension of the Gospel. These Wise Men, who were probably from Persia, were searching the higher truth.

The word 'Magi' may mean wise, but it also incorporates a sense of greatness and power. They were clearly Wise Men of importance. They must have been recognised as important leaders, but they caused quite a stir with the local people, such that Herod was involved. The message helps us to realise that God calls the great intellects of the world, as well as the poor and the ordinary. It also tells us that the gospel message is for all nations and not just for the Jews. This has been an inspiring message for Christians to become missionaries throughout the history of Christendom.

The call of all Christians is to be willing to share this message to those who are willing to hear. This is what makes the Magi stand out in their uniqueness. Despite all their wisdom and wealth, they were still seeking.

'Where is the one who has been born King of the Jews?'

The Magi showed great persistence in searching for the truth. This is a quality that Christians should emulate. Too often we can plateau in our faith and accept second best, be it for ourselves or for others who need our help. They were also willing to learn from a variety of sources, be it the Scribes and Priests, or even Herod. Here we see men with a good, godly perspective on life, which enabled them to be such wise leaders. An ability to see God's creative hand upon the world can only be a blessing to those who have eyes and ears to perceive it.

For the Magi, it was a star that led them to Christ. We will all have our own star, which acts as a catalyst and opens our eyes to Christ. For Augustine, it was a child singing, 'Take up and read'. For Brother Lawrence, it was a tree in winter waiting for spring. For some, their star was an illness, an accident, a creative revelation, the birth of a child, or a friend willing to share their story. Can you imagine, after the star stood still, the Wise Men kneeling before a camp fire, warming themselves late at night, reflecting upon their journey? They represent knowledge and learning from the breadth of the world, that leads them to be finally lost in awe and wonder.

We are all on a journey of life with key stepping stones or 'stars' that guide us. We also need moments when we pause in life and reflect where we have got up to. It provides a chance to gain a new perspective on life and perceive the way ahead. As we embrace and uphold the Christian message, may it lead us to times of awe and wonder.

Reflection

- What is the 'star' that led you to God and the manger?

- What is God calling you to be persistent in?

Prayer

Lord Jesus Christ, as I reflect on the Wise Men
with their gifts of gold, myrrh and incense,
I wonder what I can offer you?
As small as it may seem,
I pray you may use me for the good of your kingdom,
as I seek to follow your star, wherever it may lead.
Amen.

Day 18

Luke 1:46-56

We all have our own favourite part of what makes Christmas special for us. As a minister, it is seeing the church full at Christmas Eve for a Christingle service, a Nativity or a carol service. Here you have both the church congregation and community coming together. You can look around and see familiar faces from baptisms, weddings and funerals. The entire pastoral needs of a parish come together, as we sing carols of the wonder of Christmas. Here, all our own personal narratives become entwined with the story of Jesus. Bit by bit we are taken higher in wonder, awe and mystery as we offer ourselves to God in song.

This moment of being uplifted captures a flavour of what Luke provides for us in the prophetic songs of Zechariah, Mary and Simeon. These three songs capture God's heart desire and delight in his creation. The coming of Christ was not focused on judgement but on God wanting to see his creation and to be able to say, 'It is good.'

Mary reveals a deep understanding and insight into God, as he had been revealed in the Old Testament. Such a young girl, yet she grasped the character of God better than many theologians. Mary had faith to see God working quietly as the baby developed in her womb. Nine months of what appears to be inaction results in the miracle of the unique baby being born.

This is a picture of God at work, which Jesus echoes in his parables and analogies. So many of Jesus' stories related to the slow, hidden work of his creativity. He talked about the seed growing under the ground, the smallest seed producing the greatest tree, and the harvest ripening without people recognising it. Mary knew God worked in his own mysterious way. Within this plan, God's part has always been for the poor, the humble, the hungry and the helpless. What does this tell us of the character of God? How does God view us? What does he expect of us?

If this makes you feel vulnerable, then hold on to Mary's assured knowledge that God remembers and fulfils his promises. Right from the very first spoken word in creation, the call of Abraham to the coming of Jesus, God the Father has been at work fulfilling his word. If there is any doubt that we are brought to Jesus' ministry and suffering to find triumph at the cross, here God reveals that he has been found weighed in the balance and found worthy. All of this is revealed through this young girl, no wonder she was called blessed. But the joy of the Magnificat is that the blessing is not just for Mary. Verse 55 tells us that it is for all generations, if they will listen.

Reflection

- When do you feel close to God, and are you ever caught up in wonder?

- How does the Magnificat change your attitude to yourself and to God?

- What does Mary teach you about your life?

Prayer

Father, forgive me that too often
I am not caught up in the
wonder of your creative world.
Open my eyes to what you have provided for me,
so that I too might engage in your work
of caring for the poor and the hungry.
Lord, help me to be creative right to the very end of
my life.
Amen.

Day 19

Luke 1:57-66

As a teenager, I would help sail some small racing yachts, where I would lean out over the side on a trapeze wire to enable the yacht to keep on track and counteract the force of the wind. It would take very little wind to blow the boat off track. It takes nerve and determination to rely on a thin wire and lean out into the mid-air. This is a good picture of the Christian life. It is so easy to be blown by the wind of current fashions, especially at Christmas time and to follow the crowd. We follow the wide path, just like many before us. However, Jesus offered a different way, a narrow path, which wouldn't be easy, but promised the joy of God's blessing.

The question is often before us of whether we are just following the crowd, or following the Spirit's call. Zechariah found himself in just that position. The tradition of his community and family dictated that he should call the first born after the father. One could imagine the family and congregation's reaction when Elizabeth spoke out against this norm. Having a woman speak out in that way was unusual in a male-dominated culture but perhaps accepted since Zechariah had unfortunately been struck dumb. However, with the family's misfortune, surely it wasn't time to break with tradition? Zechariah followed the call of the angel and his faith, which beckoned him to follow what he believed to be right. How often do we find ourselves caught in a situation where the loudest person in the group is conveying a message which we do not believe? Do we speak out, or do we remain silent?

Reflection

- Can you think of a situation where you remained silent?

- How can you express your faith this Christmas through word or deed?

Prayer

Father, forgive me for the times I hide my faith
and too often keep silent.
Give me courage in my convictions
to express to those around me
what Christmas means to me.
Amen.

Day 20

Luke 1:67-80

Have you noticed how Luke places great importance on the birth of John the Baptist? You might wonder why, when the main event is surely the birth of Christ? Yet there is precedent. Throughout the Old Testament we find that there is often a pre-runner to a significant introduction to a person or event. Take the story of Samuel, who led the way for David. Samuel and John have similar accounts. Both were born from a barren mother, the Angel Gabriel spoke to them with 'Good News' and pronounced what name to give the child. Samuel and John were significant people in themselves but filled with the Holy Spirit, they were seen as 'great' in the Lord's eyes. Yet they were not the main event, as they were also called to prepare the way for another.

The song of Zechariah traces the hand of God through time, right back to Abraham and the covenant. Just as in genealogies, here we see God works through his people to fulfil his aims (verse 72). This plan involves the call to repentance, forgiveness and the knowledge of salvation (verse 77). Through this work, light will shine on people to bring them peace. What a calling! We don't often see ourselves perhaps in Samuel or John the Baptist's role, yet without them, we would not have had King David or the opening for Christ.

Perhaps we might wonder whether our calling is one of preparing the way for others? Could we become a significant 'other' that makes all the difference in someone's life? How special it must be to play a small role in a person's life that could change the history of humankind. Could that be you? We won't know unless we choose to actively enable individuals, by mentoring and drawing out their gifts.

Reflection

- Can you think of two or three individuals you could take under your wing and nurture?

- Begin to commit yourself in prayer for these people.

Prayer

Lord Jesus, thank you that you show us
that we all need mentors and guides
to help us on our journey of life.
Please equip us to be more giving of ourselves,
that it might enable others to find their fulfilment,
perhaps even at the expense of ourselves.
Amen.

Day 21

Luke 2:1-7

I love going to the Minack Amphitheatre in Cornwall, where you sit looking out and the backcloth of the stage is the sea. Below is the stage with all the props laid out, ready to be brought to life by the actors. In Luke Chapter 2, the stage scene is set, revealing all that there is to come in the life of Jesus. The backcloth is God's creative, on-going plan. Various props are scattered on the stage, or just lying ready to be unfolded at the appropriate moment.

Firstly, we see how the whole world is drawn into the birth of God's son. The current world government played their part through the Census decreed by Caesar Augustus. This allowed Jesus to be born in Bethlehem in the house of David. It reminds us how our Lord is so concerned with the world's affairs.

Secondly, we also see how the history of the Old Testament began to be fulfilled and the Angel Gabriel's words unfolded. Jesus reminds us later in his life that nothing will be left unfulfilled from his word. He assures us that his plan will be developed and completed.

Thirdly, we see how the time came, yet the world was still not prepared. So the baby was laid in a manger, off-stage in a quiet backwater, in a sleepy village. Just like today, we can be so busy that we miss what God is doing, right in our midst.

Fourthly, we see how the incarnate child had no home to lay his head. This reveals how far God was willing to go to allow humankind to see how committed he was to identifying with us. Only one like us, in every way, could represent us. Just like Moses, who had to leave his rich home to identity with his people Israel, Christ descended from heaven to be with his people, that he might scoop us up into his heavenly glory.

Here was the beginning of Jesus' journey into poverty and simplicity. He became a man with no home, with only one garment to wear or, as he himself put it, 'Foxes have holes, and birds of the air have nests; but the Son of Man has nowhere to lay his head' (Luke 9:58).

Finally, we see a scene of love with a young girl wrapping her cloth and arms around a vulnerable baby. Love is at the heart of the Christmas scene, the love of God for his creation and the free choice for humanity to love the creator. There is a cost for Mary to love this child, but she chose not to hold back.

Reflection

- Pray for God's hand upon the world's affairs and governments.

- Give thanks that God knows your past and future and be open to God's Spirit speaking to you today.

- Recognise how materially rich we are and see if you can help another at this time of the year.

- Pause and acknowledge the love in your life. Be willing to receive love as well as give it.

Prayer

Jesus, I thank you that you understand
and yet still care for me.
I rejoice at the extent you have travelled
to convey your message.
May I sense and accept your love around me.
Open now my heart wide to follow your example of love.
In your name.
Amen.

Day 22

Luke 2:8-18

The story of the shepherds tells us that the message of Jesus' birth was not just for the elite or special people. This message has the ability to spread out like light in the darkness. The light begins to attract attention far and wide. The first thing we discover about the shepherds was that they were terrified. Not an unfamiliar reaction for many people when you talk about religion.

Today religion can be seen as dangerous, divisive and to be avoided at all costs. The light can be twisted and diverted to appear as something that is not wholesome and healthy. We all need to be wise about anything that makes us fearful. Fear comes about because of danger, perhaps reminding us of other occasions when we have felt afraid. But we do not feel fear when we are safe and secure. When we have our 'safe base' we can relax, explore and play in life. The shepherds knew all about the fear and dangers of the night; they were on the lookout for robbers and wolves. But the 'host of angels' came and directed them to a vision of the future.

This is the message of our faith, one of hope and love. It is also a sign for people to see beyond religion. To ignore how people twist it and manipulate it for their own ends, to gaze beyond and wonder at the pure presence of God in our midst. On seeing this baby, the shepherds' hearts were lifted up and transformed. This is the fruit of any true, godly message: is it oppressive and destructive or does it liberate and bring peace for the good of others?

The result for the shepherds was an overwhelming one of release from fear, as they went about informing others of this 'Good News'. Just as the yeast raises the flour dough or the tiniest seed quietly grows into the greatest of trees, so the kingdom of God spreads with this message of love for humankind. Here we see natural evangelism from our liberated hearts, where fear has been removed, and we share this simple discovery with others.

Reflection

- When do you feel safe and secure?

- What drives away your fear?

- What 'good news' can you share with another?

Prayer

Father, open my eyes afresh to your love in my life that I might be released from that which frustrates and inhibits me.
Let my heart leap with joy that it may spill over to others.
For the gospel's sake.
Amen.

Day 23

Luke 2:19

My wife gave me a small silver cross when we were married, which had the words of Matthew 28:20b on the back:

> 'Lo, I shall be with you always, even to the end of the age.'
> *(Amplified Bible)*

It is a verse that reminds us God will always be close. Sometimes in Scripture, it is not long monologues or accounts that speak to us, but a simple verse that we hold dear. Here, Luke speaks volumes about Mary in only a few words. Unlike the shepherds, Mary seemed less amazed. She had, of course, absorbed the message of the good news through the Angel Gabriel and her cousin Elizabeth. She also had nine months to ruminate over what this story could mean for her family and the wider world.

The verse tells us that she treasured up and pondered these things. Mary had many things to reflect upon in her life. Some events could have disheartened her and perhaps disturbed her enough to attempt to prevent his journey to the cross. Mary proved her faithfulness by being there at the end and having to look at her son hanging in agony on a cross. What a test of faith.

Can any of us reflect upon our lives and think we have had to cope with Mary's account? Just think of some of the problems she had to handle: encountering angels, becoming pregnant without intercourse, a fiancé thinking about ending their relationship, family and community rejection, no home, strange visitors, being a refugee, the massacre of similar-aged children, living in an alien country, losing a son in a big city, people questioning her son's behaviour, hearing strange accounts about her son, knowing that great authorities were concerned and watching her son, seeing crowds praise her son, yet be frightened of the religious authorities, and finally seeing her son betrayed, rejected, deserted and having to suffer the worst of deaths.

Mary, like Job, had much to bear in life. They were both changed by their experience, but held onto their belief in a mysterious, yet loving and all-powerful God. Wow! Perhaps it makes our own journey of faith seem tame in comparison but it should also give us great encouragement. Whatever our story may be, we can reflect, ponder and seek to see it through 'faithful' eyes, such that we complete the race and win the prize.

Reflection

- Can you see God walking beside you in your darker moments?

- What do Job and Mary teach you about your faith?

- What are your reflections on your life? Could you try and see your life from a different perspective?

Prayer

Lord, help me to hold onto my faith
regardless of the journey that I experience.
May I deepen my knowledge of you
and grow in my relationship of trust and hope.
Amen.

Day 24

Luke 2:21-24

As Mary continues to ponder events unfolding before her, Luke is keen to inform us of an important message of the Christian faith. First we are told that Mary and Joseph seek to comply with the Jewish law. They take their firstborn to be circumcised and presented in the temple of the Lord. This is in fulfilment of Leviticus 12:1-8, which calls for circumcision, the naming of the child and purification of Mary. There is no mention of the ritual of Exodus 13:1, 2, where Moses is told by God to consecrate every firstborn to God, in a tradition that the parents buy back their child with an offering. Although Luke's passage does remind us of a previous event with Hannah and Samuel, where Hannah fulfils her promise of giving her son to the temple as an offering of thanks (1 Samuel 1).

Here, the parents of Jesus already know clearly that this baby never really belonged to them but always belonged to God the Father. This is later revealed at Jesus' baptism where Jesus hears the Father reassure him that he is his 'beloved son'. So Joseph and Mary fulfil the Law but they also fulfil the grace given to them. At the naming, they give their baby not the name of the father, but the name given to them by the Angel Gabriel. Here we see the balance between following the word of God and the message of the Holy Spirit.

Today, as Christians, we follow the Word and seek to obey the Ten Commandments and the gospel message through the Scriptures. We apply the intelligence and learning that God the creator has given us to the text. Christians often talk about resting faith on the three-legged stool of Scripture, church history and reason. All of this directs us today, so that we are balanced believers. But we must also be open to the Holy Spirit that speaks to us today in the context of our lives. Without Mary and Joseph listening to the holy presence of the angel, we wouldn't have the gospel today.

Reflection

- How do you balance Scripture, church history and reason in your life?

- On Christmas Eve, can you set a time aside to be open to God and to allow the Holy Spirit to speak to you?

Prayer

Father, open my heart as I approach Christmas Day.
May I be thankful for all that
you have given to humankind
through the history of time.
May I recognise your presence in my life
and give me the assurance that you know my future.
Amen.

Day 25

John 1:1-14

Christmas Day is for many a time to gather together with family, food, presents and hopefully a fun-filled day. It is quite different from the first day of Jesus' birth. It was more a time of trying to survive. Few had possessions, food was scarce, and the authorities couldn't be trusted, with Herod killing wherever he willed. However, Christmas was initiated by 'another' that seemed far off. Here, it is God himself who initiated Christmas, that we might look and see God as a vulnerable baby. Here, God holds open house. We rejoice on this day that we can know something of God through his son, Jesus. It is as if God the Father is saying, 'If you want to know my character, then look, here is my signature.'

Christmas opens up to us an account of wonder as we reflect on Jesus' life, his teaching, miracles and commitment to head to the cross and resurrection. Many years ago, there was a TV medical programme called 'Your life in their hands'. But here, we see God telling us that Christmas is 'God's life in our hands'. God not only lets himself be known through Jesus, he allows his son to be accessible to all. There is more, for in the name of Jesus, the gospel writers tell us that 'God will save his people'.

At Christmas, the pure white candles and the royal colours, the sumptuous generosity of the feasting, all come at a price. God's glory, peace and joy are not shiny wrapping paper, taped over a throwaway gift. They encompass God's grace and truth in a world marred by selfishness, greed, pain and war. Jesus' birth revealed God's glory and the beginning of peace between heaven and humanity. That's why it causes us even now to wonder and to worship, if we have but eyes to see.

Reflection

- What is it about the birth of Christ that fills you with awe and wonder?

Prayer

Lord, open my heart to wonder and amazement.
May your birth fill me with joy and thanksgiving.
I thank you that you know me,
forgive me and enable me to seek fulfilment in my life.
May I rest in your peace and,
in times of painful turmoil,
see the glory through the 'grey'.
Amen.

Day 26

Luke 2:25-40

Simeon is a fascinating character that Luke introduces us to. He tells us three times that this old man was open to the Holy Spirit. Simeon's prophetic ability enabled him to recognise that this babe in Mary's arms was the Messiah. Prophecy is not just about speaking out, but an ability to recognise and discern the situation. This requires us to be in the right place at the right time and to interpret the situation. As Simeon holds the baby there is an 'Ah-ha!' moment when Simeon realises the significance of this child. Simeon's heart is uplifted and filled with such peace that he begins to praise God. But what did he perceive?

Simeon's first words tell us so much. Now he knows, he can die in peace. Here in his arms is the hope that humanity has been waiting for. Contained in this tiny life force was the potential for bringing a light for all people, both Jews and Gentiles. No wonder Simeon could face death with peace. Simeon's prayer and praise is still unfolding as God's salvation works out in the life of humankind.

Mary and Joseph were amazed at Simeon's words. Perhaps they had thought Jesus was only going to be significant for the Jewish nation. But the message is not that simple. For Simeon goes on to give a mixed message to the family. This child's message will force both Jew and Gentile to decide their fate. Will they accept him and follow his way or reject him? And for Mary herself, Simeon sees only hard pain and the shadow of the cross.

What does this passage teach us for today? Our calling is to perceive, like Simeon, that which is before us. What would bring us such peace that we could then allow death to knock on our door? Can we grasp the significance of salvation in our lives, that whatever happens, we can find God's *Shalom* in the situation? Perhaps the passage highlights to us the importance (in a fast-moving world) that we may be missing out, if we are not willing to listen to the elders of our community.

Reflection

- How can the gospel bring you peace in the context of your life?

- Is there an elderly person who could be a blessing to you?

Prayer

Father, I thank you for the older generation that I, one day will join.
Help me to respect and care for them
and be open to their words of wisdom.
Amen.

Day 27

Matthew 2:13-18

We have become increasingly aware of what it means to be a refugee and to travel to a strange country, hoping to find a friendly welcome and support. As we have seen with Syrian refugees, the experience can often be traumatic. We are unaware of what it was like for Jesus' family to travel to Egypt for fear of their lives, but we do know it was just as problematic in Bethlehem. Once Herod realised that the Magi had tricked him, he retaliated with rage and destruction. We cannot imagine what it was like to be caught in the wave of revenge. What we do know is that pain and suffering knocks on everyone's door at some point in their life.

How does our faith respond in such a time? For some people their faith remains static. After all, we know there are consequences if we break the fundamental rules of life. Unhealthy living will naturally shorten lives. If a son speeds and crashes his car and dies, a parent might conclude that it only affirms their faith that there is a consequence to our behaviour. Others find that they have to redefine their faith and spirituality. God becomes less of a 'genie' who answers prayers but they still pray for comfort and hope. This spiritual shift might result in a change of church, or for a few, a change to a different denomination or even religion. Others find that pain challenges their faith, yet at the same time deepens and renews it. Is this what happened to Job or C. S. Lewis?

We don't know how the people of Bethlehem coped with the death of their children, or the impact it made when Mary and Joseph heard of this event. All we can do is be wise enough to develop a robust faith that copes with whatever the world throws at us.

Perhaps art can teach us something about suffering. An artist chooses a particular canvas and types of paint to work with. Once chosen, he or she has to adapt according to the conditions, along with the limitations of the material at hand. The artist's problems may not be the result of their ability, but from the limitation of the paints, colours and texture of the canvas. A good artist doesn't give up but keeps working on areas where things have gone wrong, seeking improvement. In the same way, God has chosen his creation (with its strengths of free will) and the consequences that this involves. Terrible things can and do occur, but God is still at work as Father, Son and Holy Spirit, seeking healing and redemption.

Reflection

- How can you welcome the 'Mary and Josephs' in our community?

- How can you weep with those who weep but still have hope?

- How can you have faith that is resilient to whatever befalls us?

Prayer

Father, my hearts ache for those less fortunate than myself.
As I approach a new year,
help me to be more caring for those in need
and more understanding that 'there but for the grace of
God go I'.
Amen.

Day 28

Luke 2:41-52

Working in a university, I love the student graduation ceremony. It is such a celebratory occasion with graduates, surrounded by family and friends. It is a time when we give thanks for lessons learnt, struggles overcome, appreciate those who have travelled on the journey and hope for what lies ahead. Graduation feels like the climax of a pilgrimage, taking three to four years.

Luke tells us Jesus learnt very early on in his life what it was to travel on a pilgrimage.

The Old Testament Hebrews embarked on a pilgrimage to the high city of Jerusalem. Along the way they would sing the Songs of Ascents, (Psalms 120-134). These Psalms reminded them of their history, the struggles of those of faith and the hopes before them. This is the setting that Jesus is brought up with when his parents took him to Jerusalem.

Here he is as a boy, learning his history, also with the hope of what was yet to come. Jesus amazed the leaders of the day with his knowledge of God. Yet this wasn't enough, Jesus was on a journey not just of human maturity and wisdom but a journey embracing the Father's presence, through the Spirit, bringing something new to life. Joseph and Mary were confused when they lost Jesus, but he seemed to know exactly where he was when he said, 'I am in my Father's house.' Not that he stayed there, but returned to his parents to work out his manhood in a carpenter's home.

We can find ourselves oscillating from Sunday in church to grappling with the week ahead of work, family and daily pressures. We all need special moments in 'my Father's house'. Alas, with Sunday trading and busy lives, we can easily get caught up with everything from the working week that squeezes out Sabbath rest, worship and prayer. Jesus met leaders in the temple, who were well behind his level of knowledge, but he didn't remain there, he pushed on in his understanding of God to fulfil his Father's will.

This is a challenge to us all, in not becoming complacent in what we have learned in our faith, but to go on seeking a deeper maturity of belief and pursuing Christian action.

Reflection

- How can you go up and meet God on Sunday? What do you expect from your Sunday worship?

- Do you need to book in special moments to acknowledge your pilgrimage journey?

- Are you like the teachers who seemed to have reached a plateau or are you still growing in faith?

Prayer

Jesus, give me a thirst to understand your ways,
that I will never be complacent
but push on in my understanding of your word
to stretch my faith.
Amen.

Day 29

Matthew 2:19-23

We can only imagine what it was like for Mary and Joseph with baby Jesus in the first few years of their family life. Their toil was not a lot different from many today who struggle to make ends meet. It is so easy to get lost in the pain of daily life. However, we do know that they did not lose faith in their God. Joseph was still open enough to discern another godly dream and act upon it. This doesn't mean his decision to return home was easy. As they started their homeward journey, Joseph had second thoughts and was filled with doubt. How reassuring that we see the human side of Joseph. Yet even here, God was at work and led them to Nazareth.

Life in our fast-moving commercial and advertising world is just as complex. We have often been sold a subliminal message of life, which says that you must know everything that's happening right now (no wonder we are anxious and exhausted); you must have all the toys now (no wonder we're in debt); everything should be quick, easy and successful (no wonder we have more depression, broken relationships and failed businesses). It is hard to follow God if you still believe something contradictory. Many Christians struggle on with their daily tussles of life, wondering why their life is flat and they are ill at ease. What have we been telling ourselves that is just not true? We end up with a belief system that we have not directly chosen.

People can tell you that they don't believe in anything, but with a little scratching at the surface, you soon find out they believe in all kinds of moralistic views, which may be good or bad but fail to have any roots or foundations. When they enter difficulties in life, these beliefs are too shallow to sustain them or guide them.

If we are consistently to follow God, who is 'the way, the truth and the life', it might involve taking a fresh look at our life style and perhaps letting go of wrong thoughts, ways and beliefs. We all require deep roots of faith if we are to cope with all the winds and waves of the world that get thrown at us.

Reflection

- In your daily life, what things make you anxious?

- What do you use to guide you in your decisions of life?

- How can you prevent yourself from making foolish decisions?

Prayer

Lord, I get so quickly caught up in the worries of the day that I find myself anxious and unsettled.
Please enable me to focus on what is important
and not be so easily distracted.

Help me to base my thinking on your word,
my feelings controlled by my prayer life
and my actions guided by those I trust.
Amen.

Day 30

Matthew 3:13-17

John the Baptist has now grown up and has commenced his ministry. It certainly wasn't a conventional approach and if his parents were still alive, it might not have been what they had expected. John had developed his own way of thinking and expectations. When he finally met Jesus, he assumed it would be Jesus the Messiah who would baptise him. But Jesus corrects his thinking. Jesus focuses upon righteousness and his reward is to hear his heavenly Father tell him that 'he is loved and is pleasing to his Father'.

Making the right decisions in life is clearly not easy. Despite John's life of prayer and preparation, he was still capable of being off the mark. Modern life is just as complex. The scatter effect of the brain means that we have thousands of butterfly-like thoughts every day fluttering into our view. Which butterfly thought do we choose to catch and follow? They are just thoughts that initially are all neutral. But they can also be packed with a powerful punch if we hold onto them and allow them to take root. Christian growth requires an ability to begin to discern what is good and honourable. We have to recognise when we are focusing on unhealthy thinking. The butterfly thoughts that we hold onto will affect our feelings, which in turn affect our behaviour.

Jesus could have easily assumed authority over John and lorded it over him, but he chose humility and was rewarded accordingly. How many times did Jesus hold onto the words given to him by his Father? If you keep thinking you are loved by God and that he is pleased with you and wants the best for your life, such thoughts will inevitably lead to positive feelings and positive behaviour in your life. Our self-esteem or self-worth can be a very fluid thing and depend on the circumstances of our lives. However, if we hold onto God's Word, that he has made us in his image, forgives and seeks us to reach our potential, surely it will guide our thoughts, feelings and actions?

Reflection

- How can you let go of negative thinking?
- How can you shape your thinking around God's Word?
- Can you recognise the triggers that make you anxious?
- What positive things can you focus upon?

Prayer

Lord, show me the depth of your love for me,
that it might be the foundation of my life.
Help me to let go of the thoughts that are not of you
and focus and hold onto righteous, godly thinking
and behaviour.
Amen.

Day 31

Matthew 4:1-11

Thirty years have now gone by in Jesus' life, of which we know so little. But perhaps this gives us a message. Why is it that God does not tell us about Jesus' routine life as a teenager, as a young man, learning his father's trade, perhaps coping with the death of a father and supporting his mother and his brothers and sisters? Does this emulate our own lives? After all, our lives flash by, so often with little significance.

We too can meander through a thirty-year period and question whether God was with us. However, perhaps in the silence, it reminds us that God is with us through the mundane, everyday factors of life. We don't need to know all of the detail of Jesus' early life, except we know that God in the flesh understands what it means to be human and to live a very ordinary life. Has God been with us through the many stages of our life? Surely the answer is yes?

After thirty years of waiting, Jesus began his ministry in perhaps an unexpected way. It was the Holy Spirit who guided him into the desert, even though it led to a time of temptation. He spent forty days and forty nights grappling with 'the way, the truth and the life'. Firstly, it was turning stone to bread – after all, he would have been very hungry. Then, it was using his power as a 'convincer' of his identity. Finally, it was committing himself to something selfish that he had to resist. At the end of this ordeal, Jesus wasn't left alone, but was attended to by God's angels.

As we begin a new year tomorrow, we too are like Jesus, about to begin a new period of our lives. It is just another day, month, year, but it can also be a catalyst to reflect upon a changed perspective in our lives. New year resolutions tend not to last long, unless we are determined and have support. What we don't know is what life will throw at us. However, we can make up our mind, like Jesus, to be prepared.

Trials and tribulations come to us all, but the Psalmist reminds us that God can be in all places. Psalm 139 tells us that whatever happens in life, God can and will be with us. This tells us that we can find God in all situations, in times of great joy, and in times of illness and loneliness. Surely, if God is God, if we are open to him, we will find him in every situation?

Reflection

- How can you find God in times of darkness and difficulty?

- How can you be prepared for whatever life might throw at you in this coming year?

Prayer

Father, in this New Year may I praise you,
for you have fearfully and wonderfully made me.

May I marvel in your works that my soul might know you in all I do
and whatever befalls me.
So go with me in my thoughts, words and deeds throughout this New Year.
Amen.